Presented to

_____

by

_____

on

_____

What Every Mother Must Teach Her Children

Clarence Sexton

Fourth Edition
April 2007

CROWN
CHRISTIAN
PUBLICATIONS
Royal Reading

P.O. Box 159
Powell, Tennessee 37849

1-877 AT CROWN

Dedicated To My Mother

Ruby Lee

As the oldest of four children, I enjoyed a lot of attention from my mother, especially as a young boy.

So many precious memories flood my soul as I think about my mother. She was used of God to plant the thought in my heart that the Lord had a special purpose for my life. She expected me to always put forth my very best effort.

When as a young teen I trusted the Lord Jesus Christ as my personal Savior; my mother was the very first person with whom I shared the news. She met me at the door, and I said, "Mother, I was saved tonight. I trusted Jesus Christ as my Savior." She replied, "That's good," and she hugged me. As she turned to walk back into the room, after taking a step or two, she turned back to me and said, "No, that's very good!"

When I was just a child, my mother spoke with me often on a wide range of subjects. She gave instruction on everything from steering clear of bad habits to what colors matched in the clothing I wore.

Certain words and expressions were never allowed to come from our lips. For example, we were never to use the word *fool* or the expression, *shut up*. We were always to answer adults as sir or ma'am, and of course we could never talk back to an adult. Respect was very important. Mother taught us that we were special, and while other children might be allowed to run wild, her children were going to do right and honor God.

My mother was far from being a perfect woman, but she loved her children. She knew that God gave us to her, and she spent time teaching us to do right.

The thoughts you find in this book are dedicated to my darling mother with a prayer that the influence she had on me will help you to be more of what God intends for you to be.

Proverbs 31

1   *The words of king Lemuel, the prophecy that his mother taught him.*

2   *What, my son? and what, the son of my womb? and what, the son of my vows?*

3   *Give not thy strength unto women, nor thy ways to that which destroyeth kings.*

4   *It is not for kings, O Lemuel, it is not for kings to drink wine; nor for princes strong drink:*

5   *Lest they drink, and forget the law, and pervert the judgment of any of the afflicted.*

6   *Give strong drink unto him that is ready to perish, and wine unto those that be of heavy hearts.*

7   *Let him drink, and forget his poverty, and remember his misery no more.*

8   *Open thy mouth for the dumb in the cause of all such as are appointed to destruction.*

9   *Open thy mouth, judge righteously, and plead the cause of the poor and needy.*

10 *Who can find a virtuous woman? for her price is far above rubies.*

        11   *The heart of her husband doth safely trust in her, so that he shall have no need of spoil.*

        12 *She will do him good and not evil all the days of her life.*

        13 *She seeketh wool, and flax, and worketh willingly with her hands.*

"Who can find a virtuous woman?"
Proverbs 31:10

14 She is like the merchants' ships; she bringeth her food from afar.

15 She riseth also while it is yet night, and giveth meat to her household, and a portion to her maidens.

16 She considereth a field, and buyeth it: with the fruit of her hands she planteth a vineyard.

17 She girdeth her loins with strength, and strengtheneth her arms.

18 She perceiveth that her merchandise is good: her candle goeth not out by night.

19 She layeth her hands to the spindle, and her hands hold the distaff.

20 She stretcheth out her hand to the poor; yea, she reacheth forth her hands to the needy.

21 She is not afraid of the snow for her household: for all her household are clothed with scarlet.

22 She maketh herself coverings of tapestry; her clothing is silk and purple.

23 Her husband is known in the gates, when he sitteth among the elders of the land.

24 She maketh fine linen, and selleth it; and delivereth girdles unto the merchant.

25 Strength and honour are her clothing; and she shall rejoice in time to come.

26 She openeth her mouth with wisdom; and in her tongue is the law of kindness.

27 She looketh well to the ways of her household, and eateth not the bread of idleness.

28 Her children arise up, and call her blessed; her husband also, and he praiseth her.

29 Many daughters have done virtuously, but thou excellest them all.

30 Favour is deceitful, and beauty is vain: but a woman that feareth the Lord, she shall be praised.

31 Give her of the fruit of her hands; and let her own works praise her in the gates.

TABLE OF CONTENTS

In chapter one and verse one of Proverbs, the Bible says these are *"the proverbs of Solomon the son of David, king of Israel."* In the first chapter, a father instructs his son. In the last chapter, chapter thirty-one, we find a mother instructing her son.

Let us consider what mothers must teach their children. This mother told her son what he must know one item at a time. God gave me a mother who was keenly interested in the matter of instructing her children. Every mother desires certain things for her children; but it is the Lord, and only the Lord, who gives clear direction and discernment to a mother concerning where to place the emphasis in the matter of instructing her children. Each mother must seek to follow the Lord in order to instruct her children properly.

Imagine a mother seated by her son giving these words of wisdom, instructing him and telling him things that he must hear. These are things that a mother must teach her children.

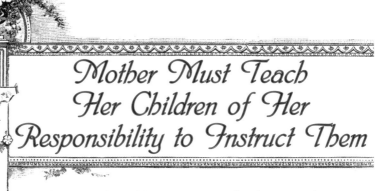

Mother Must Teach Her Children of Her Responsibility to Instruct Them

1

> *"The words of king Lemuel, the prophecy that his mother taught him."*
>
> Proverbs 31:1

As we begin in Proverbs chapter thirty-one, working our way through it verse by verse, the Bible says, *"The words of king Lemuel, the prophecy that his mother taught him."* The very first thing Mother must do is tell her children that she is responsible to teach them. The Bible says, *"The words of king Lemuel, the prophecy that his mother taught him."* There is no pretense here about who is responsible. Oh, what power rests in a mother's words and deeds!

We know very little about King Lemuel. Some have the idea that this may be a name for Solomon. The instruction given is from a godly woman to a son who becomes king. If this king is King Solomon, then his mother was none other than Bathsheba. What a marvelous work of the grace of God that He worked in the life of this mother.

I am so very grateful to God for the grace He clearly demonstrated in my mother's life as she trusted Christ as her personal Savior. The transformation in her life was evident.

The Bible says of this mother that she told her son in the very outset of chapter thirty-one, "It is my responsibility to tell you these things." Her responsibility cannot be assigned to someone else. It is not a responsibility to be given to the school. It is not a responsibility to be given to the church. It is a responsibility that a mother knows God has given to her. This mother told her son in the very beginning, "These are things that I must tell you." Mothers need not seek to make a list of priorities for their children; they should simply seek to follow the clear teaching of God's Word found here.

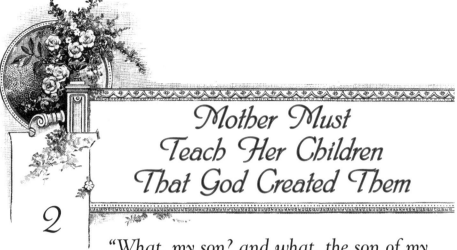

Mother Must Teach Her Children That God Created Them

2

"What, my son? and what, the son of my womb? and what, the son of my vows?"

Proverbs 31:2

Not only did this mother tell her son that she must instruct him, she also told him from whence he came. The Bible says in verse two, *"What, my son? and what, the son of my womb? and what, the son of my vows?"* She explained to her son how he came to be.

All of us know that our children are going to be bombarded with false teaching and lies about where they came from, especially as we think about the subject of evolution. But here we find a mother seated with her son, saying to him, "You are *the son of my womb, the son of my vows"* She told this boy where he came from, that God had blessed her, and that she had been able to give birth to him. He was not a product of evolution; he was a gift from God, divinely created, brought forth from his mother's womb. His mother had prayed that God would give her this son.

I would like to imagine that every Christian mother tells her children that she has a God-given responsibility to talk to them. There are clearly defined things that she must tell her children, and she should begin by telling each child that he came from God.

Only God knows how convincing the arguments may appear to be when the child is bombarded with the Devil's lies concerning how he came into being. The real battle is not won or lost in whether or not a teacher can be convincing enough in a classroom. The real battle for the child is won or lost in whether or not a mother assumes her God-given responsibility to teach her child that he came from God.

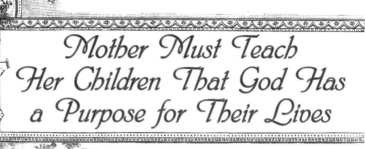

Mother Must Teach Her Children That God Has a Purpose for Their Lives

3

> "Give not thy strength unto women, nor
> thy ways to that which destroyeth kings."
> Proverbs 31:3

Thirdly, she told him that God had a plan for his life. The Bible says in verse three, *"Give not thy strength unto women, nor thy ways to that which destroyeth kings."* In other words, she said to her child, "Your life is not an accident. God has a special purpose for you." Over and over, my mother told me that God had a special purpose for my life. She was used of God to convince me that the Lord wanted my life for His glory.

Of course, the great purpose of life is to come to know the Lord Jesus as your personal Savior, to recognize that God created you for Himself, and to ask Him to forgive your sin and by faith receive the Lord Jesus as your personal Savior.

The Bible says in Ephesians chapter three and verse eleven that God has an eternal purpose. Our purpose is to find our place in His eternal purpose.

This mother said to her son, *"Give not thy strength unto women, nor thy ways to that which destroyeth kings."* God created men and women. There is a difference between a man and a woman. Children are being taught many lies about gender and gender preferences. The lies that are being propagated by the homosexual community can be combated at Mother's knee.

A mother tells her child, "God made you a little boy, and little boys have a purpose in life different from little girls." It is Mother's God-given assignment to tell each of her children, "God has a specific purpose for your life."

I grew up in a family with a brother and two sisters. Tommy and I knew that we were different than our two sisters, Katherine and Sheila. A certain modesty was always promoted by my mother toward my sisters. The boys were taught to give the highest respect to the girls. My brother and I would grow up and have wives, and my sisters would grow up and have husbands.

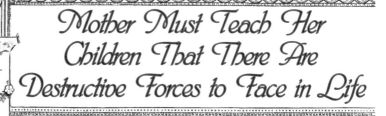

Mother Must Teach Her Children That There Are Destructive Forces to Face in Life

4

"It is not for kings, O Lemuel, it is not for kings to drink wine; nor for princes strong drink: lest they drink, and forget the law, and pervert the judgment of any of the afflicted."

Proverbs 31:4-5

She said in verses four and five, *"It is not for kings, O Lemuel, it is not for kings to drink wine; nor for princes strong drink: lest they drink, and forget the law, and pervert the judgment of any of the afflicted."*

She said, "I'm going to warn you about some things. There are specific things I need to tell you about that can destroy your life." She had boldness about it. To this idea of never letting alcohol touch the lips, Mother may add instruction about never taking drugs and never smoking cigarettes.

17

She went over this with her son saying, "These are things that can destroy your life." Sounding out warnings is a responsibility given to Mother.

As I grew up, my mother taught me that certain things would destroy my life. She made me promise her that I would not do certain things or allow the wrong things to enter my body.

"All hell cannot tear a boy or girl away from a praying mother."
-Billy Sunday

Mother Must Teach
Her Children to Show Mercy

5

"Give strong drink unto him that is ready to perish, and wine unto those that be of heavy hearts. Let him drink, and forget his poverty, and remember his misery no more."

Proverbs 31:6-7

The Bible says in verses six and seven, *"Give strong drink unto him that is ready to perish, and wine unto those that be of heavy hearts. Let him drink, and forget his poverty, and remember his misery no more."* Do not be confused by these verses. This speaks of showing mercy to those who are dying.

She said to her child, "I do not want you to be a hard-hearted person. I want you to be a caring person, a loving person, a forgiving person. I want you to realize that there are people who need mercy." She took the time to explain to her child the situations that required great mercy. Tenderness was taught by this mother to her son. We live in an age of hard-heartedness, cruelty, and unconcern. Many mothers have allowed others to care for their children. Institutions from preschool and upward may provide food and safety, but a mother's love is missing. Mother's mercy is sorely missing in today's world.

Never despair of a child. The one you weep the most for at the mercy seat may fill your heart with the sweetest joy.

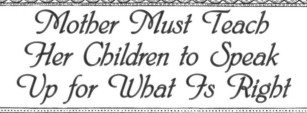

Mother Must Teach Her Children to Speak Up for What Is Right

6

> "*Open thy mouth for the dumb in the cause of all such as are appointed to destruction. Open thy mouth, judge righteously, and plead the cause of the poor and needy.*"
>
> Proverbs 31:8-9

n verses eight and nine the Bible says, "*Open thy mouth for the dumb in the cause of all such as are appointed to destruction. Open thy mouth, judge righteously, and plead the cause of the poor and needy.*"

She desired for her son to be a person who spoke up for what was right. She taught him to have the boldness and virtue to open his mouth and speak out for what is right.

We live in a world that is filled with the sin of silence. So many of us know we should lift our voices and speak out against evil, but we remain silent. So many of us know that God gives us opportunities to speak, but we do not speak. It is just as wrong not to do right as it is to march out and do wrong.

21

PRESTON AND RUBY SEXTON WITH
THEIR INFANT SON, CLARENCE

Mother Must Teach Her Children About Moral Purity

7

"Who can find a virtuous woman? for her price is far above rubies."

Proverbs 31:10

She told him of moral purity, saying in verse ten, *"Who can find a virtuous woman? for her price is far above rubies."*

Mother must deal with her children concerning the subjects of sex and marriage. She must refuse to send her son or daughter off to school somewhere and allow a teacher to teach her child what the world calls "sex education." She must take the responsibility of telling her children about moral things. She must press the point of moral purity to them, talking about virtue and moral decency. She must talk about the matter of sex and abstinence before marriage. She must explain to her daughter what a godly girl will not do and to her son what a godly boy will not do. She must explain to her son what to look for in a young lady and to her daughter what to look for in a young man. She must warn her daughter about the world in which she lives and the pressure that is going to be put on her for sexual impurity. She must not simply hope that someone will come along and speak to her children about these vital matters.

Mother Must Teach Her Children Why She Works

8

"The heart of her husband doth safely trust in her, so that he shall have no need of spoil. She will do him good and not evil all the days of her life."

Proverbs 31:11-12

This is of extreme importance. A mother must tell her children why she works. The Bible says in verse eleven, *"The heart of her husband doth safely trust in her, so that he shall have no need of spoil. She will do him good and not evil all the days of her life."*

Notice how she got into the subject of work. On her way to deal with the subject of her own labor and work, she reassured her child of her love and devotion for his father. A child needs to be reassured by his mother that she has love and loyalty toward his father. So many married couples live in fear that is created by not being able to trust one another. This mother said to her son, "I want you to know that I love your father and that I am loyal to your father."

She went as far as to say, "I am going to be faithful all the days of my life to your father. I love your father, and I intend to be loyal to your father all the days of my life." These are things a mother must tell her children.

"The heart of her husband doth safely trust in her, so that he shall have no need of spoil."

So many Christians who know God and know God's Word wait for other people to instruct their children. Our Lord has assigned parents the authority over their own children. So much heartache can be spared if the right things are done in the home. She said to her son, "I love your father. I am going to be loyal to your father."

She told him why she worked. Notice what the Bible says in verses thirteen through sixteen, *"She seeketh wool, and flax, and worketh willingly with her hands. She is like the merchants' ships; she bringeth her food from afar. She riseth also while it is yet night, and giveth meat to her household, and a portion to her maidens. She considereth a field, and buyeth it: with the fruit of her hands she planteth a vineyard."*

She explained to her son why she worked. This is so important. She told him that she was not a career woman. She was not working for herself. She was not working to achieve something for herself. She was not working because she desired the notoriety that a career brings. She was working for her son and her husband.

We have reared an entire generation of young ladies with the idea that they are never going to be what they should be unless they have a career. According to the latest surveys, only one out of every four young women in America believes she should not be pursuing a career. Half of the women in America believe that it is their responsibility in life to balance a mate, children, and a career. Only one out of every four women believes it is not her responsibility to pursue a career.

In other words, we have just about convinced women to leave their vacuum cleaners for a computer and give the office the interest that should be given to home and family. They have been convinced that they should be more concerned about what kind of office they have than what kind of home they have. They are convinced they cannot really be happy simply being a mother and having children. But women find out that God put something in them that they cannot escape. There is a greater call in their hearts for the cry of a baby than there is for all the demands of a job.

We have reared a generation that believes they cannot be happy anywhere. They cannot be happy at home. They really cannot be happy at work. They are miserably unhappy no matter what they try to do. A woman who knows God and loves God and loves her children is not a woman who pursues a career as the goal of her life. It just does not happen.

Our world is so mixed up. We are so far from what Christian people should be doing that it sounds almost rebellious for a man to state what I have just stated. Some people may even say that it is degrading to women.

Some women must work outside the home. My mother had to work outside the home. My wife's mother also had to work outside the home. My mother and father were divorced, and my father died leaving my mother the responsibility to rear four children. She had to go to work–not because she wanted a career, but because she had a family for which to provide. My wife's mother was also left with the responsibility of raising two young children after the tragic death of her husband in an automobile accident.

If you are a working mother, it is extremely important to explain to children why you are working. I never once resented that my mother was not there because I knew why she was working. If my mother had been working to establish some sort of career and to have more for herself, I would have resented every moment she was not there for me and my brother and two sisters. The things in our lives she had to miss because she worked outside the home caused no resentment in my heart because I knew why she was working. She was working for her children. If she had been working only to establish some name for herself or to pursue some career, I would have resented what she missed.

My wife's mother had to work. She worked in a school cafeteria where her children attended school — not because she wanted a career in the school cafeteria, but because she had two children she was responsible for feeding. She prayed and asked God for a job and sought employment where she could be near her children. It was not the job she was after, but she was taking care of her God-given responsibilities.

This may sound so out of step with our age, but it is true. My heart hurts for so many young ladies who say, "I've got a career. I've got an education to pursue. I can't get married while I'm young. I can't have children while I'm young." We find in our nation so many people beyond their twenties, into their thirties, and even into their forties who have tried the career route and have never had time for a family. Unfortunately, this is the way they have been reared by many mothers who believed all the lies of the radical feminists and repeated them to their children. This woman in Proverbs chapter thirty-one took time to tell her son why she was working.

You may think you have a good daycare in which to place your children; but it is an inescapable, haunting thought to think of the children lined up on mats on a concrete floor taking naps with their thumbs in their mouths, stuck in a corner somewhere waiting for Mother to get there when her job is over.

Some mother may say, "You're making me feel very guilty." I am saying to you that if you can go home and stay home, go home and stay home. If you cannot, then sit down and tell your children why you are working. This needs to be done. They will love you and not resent you for it.

Mother Must Teach Her Children to Take Care of Their Bodies

9

"She girdeth her loins with strength, and strengtheneth her arms."

Proverbs 31:17

his mother spoke about caring for the bodies the Lord gives us. Verse seventeen says, *"She girdeth her loins with strength, and strengtheneth her arms."* The emphasis here is on physical well-being. She talks to her children about their physical bodies. She tells them they should take care of their bodies because they are a gift from God. The proper emphasis is the emphasis we find in God's Word.

Where do children learn the physical things they need to know? They need to learn them from their mothers. They should be taught everything from caring for their teeth, eyes, and ears to washing properly. God has given each of us a wonderful body in which we can live and serve Him. The Bible says we are *"fearfully and wonderfully made."* A mother should tell her children to take care of their God-given bodies.

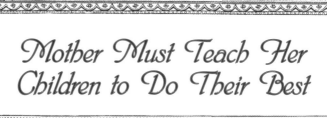

Mother Must Teach Her Children to Do Their Best

"She perceiveth that her merchandise is good: her candle goeth not out by night."
Proverbs 31:18

She spoke to him about doing his best. Verse eighteen says, *"She perceiveth that her merchandise is good: her candle goeth not out by night."* The word *perceiveth* is a word having to do with judging or testing. Not just any old thing will do for this mother's family. She wants her family to have the best. This does not mean that it is necessarily the most expensive. It means that she has such interest in her family that her children have confidence that their mother wants to feed them the right things and provide the right place for them to live. Taking the high

road in life is discerning between the good and the best–not the good and the bad–and choosing the best.

Perhaps some people are thinking that this emphasis should be coming from a father. For some reason, God starts the book of Proverbs with a father and a son; but He concludes the book of Proverbs in chapter thirty-one with a mother and her son. No one has the influence over children like a mother. There is no fit substitute in life for a mother's love and instruction. There never has been and never will be.

The truth is, children would be better off with less of this world's goods and more time with their mothers. It is not easy to say these things in our perverted world, but they need to be said. Mothers who are obedient to God work at placing in the hearts of their children a desire for the best. Be sure this is taught not only in word, but in deed.

*Home, sweet home—where each lives
for the other, and all live for God.*

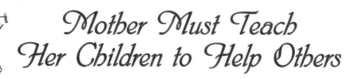

Mother Must Teach Her Children to Help Others

11

"She layeth her hands to the spindle, and her hands hold the distaff. She stretcheth out her hand to the poor; yea, she reacheth forth her hands to the needy."

Proverbs 31:19-20

Look closely at verses nineteen and twenty. *"She layeth her hands to the spindle, and her hands hold the distaff. She stretcheth out her hand to the poor; yea, she reacheth forth her hands to the needy."* Mother says to her children, "Help others."

Here is a woman who is working hard, working into the night. But she says to her children, "There are others in need, and we must reach out to help our neighbors. We are not going to live selfish lives. I am not going to rear you to think that you are the only important person in the world." Here is a mother who tells her children to care for other people and work at meeting the needs of other people. I would like for my family to live next door to someone like that. Would you not?

Through the ages, no nation has had a better friend than the mother who taught her child to pray.

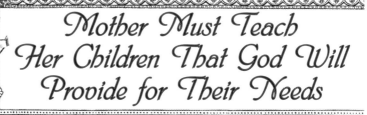

Mother Must Teach Her Children That God Will Provide for Their Needs

12

"She is not afraid of the snow for her household: for all her household are clothed with scarlet. She maketh herself coverings of tapestry; her clothing is silk and purple. Her husband is known in the gates, when he sitteth among the elders of the land. She maketh fine linen, and selleth it; and delivereth girdles unto the merchant."

Proverbs 31:21-24

The Bible says in verses twenty-one through twenty-four, *"She is not afraid of the snow for her household: for all her household are clothed with scarlet. She maketh herself coverings of tapestry; her clothing is silk and purple. Her husband is known in the gates, when he sitteth among the elders of the land. She maketh fine linen, and selleth it; and delivereth girdles unto the merchant."*

The Bible says she had no fear. Her household was provided for, and she told her children, "You don't have to worry and fret. God takes care of our needs."

There is so much fear in our world today—fear of nuclear holocaust, fear of war, fear of the collapse of our way of life. Early in life little children need to hear from Mother that God has always taken care of them and He always will. They should not have to wait to get to church to hear the preacher say it, though the preacher should say it. They need to hear Mother say, "God has always met our needs, and God always will meet our needs." Out of faith in God we find the courage to face life.

As my precious mother was dying, I said to her, "Mother, you have had a good life." She said, "No, wonderful, wonderful, wonderful. God has been so good to us. We never went hungry. He has always provided for our needs."

"She is not afraid of the snow for her household."
Proverbs 31:21

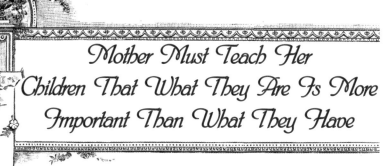

Mother Must Teach Her Children That What They Are Is More Important Than What They Have

13

"Strength and honour are her clothing;
and she shall rejoice in time to come."

Proverbs 31:25

Verse twenty-five says, *"Strength and honour are her clothing; and she shall rejoice in time to come."* She spoke of *"strength and honour."* She explained to her son that character, integrity, and decency are the essential ingredients of life. She explained to him that other people may have things they do not have, but life is not the abundance of things. Our Lord desires that we be the people He wants us to be.

She said, "Son, the kind of person you are–the decent, God-fearing, grateful, forgiving, Christ-honoring person you are is more important than everything else you'll ever have." *"Strength and honour are her clothing."* Her children were able to witness this in her life.

Thoughts on Children

Abraham Lincoln wrote, "A child is a person who is going to carry on what you have started. He will sit where you sit; and when you are gone, attend to those things which you think are important. He will control your cities, states, and nations. He will move in and take over your churches, schools, and corporations. The fate of humanity is in his hands."

Alice V. Keller said, "Everyone who touches the life of a child contributes in some way to the person he becomes. The quality of our society does not emerge accidentally. We create it. In large measure it lies in the children who will become the adult generation.

"The breakdown of the home is a national tragedy. No wonder many young boys and girls are delinquent–they have poor home lives. They eat out of the refrigerator. Family members keep different hours. Children need caring parents. They need a mother and a father they can look up to, whom they can honor. They need leadership that will reliably guide them on the pathway of life.

"Christian education should help fortify Christian homes. Your children are your most important asset. They are more important than new furniture or a new car. They will rise up and call you blessed if properly trained; or they will be the source of your greatest heartache, if not. It does not cost to train your child scripturally; it pays."

Mother Must Teach Her Children to Speak the Truth in Love

14

"She openeth her mouth with wisdom;
and in her tongue is the law of kindness."
Proverbs 31:26

he Bible says in verse twenty-six, *"She openeth her mouth with wisdom; and in her tongue is the law of kindness."* Note the words *"wisdom"* and *"kindness."*

She said to her son, "It is not enough to say the right thing; you must say it in the right way." Speak the truth; but speak the truth in love, wisdom, and kindness. The Bible says in Ephesians chapter four and verse fifteen, *"Speaking the truth in love."*

Many men and women have right things to say, but they certainly do not say them the right way. A loving mother who knows the Lord must tell her children that they not only need to know the truth and speak the truth, they must speak the truth in love. Many times my mother said to me, "When leading people, you must meet them where they are; and then lead them where you want them to be." There will always be someone who is ready to listen to the person who has been taught to speak the truth in love.

The best time to spend on your children is your time.

Mother Must Teach Her Children to Be Blessings to Their Families

15

"She looketh well to the ways of her household, and eateth not the bread of idleness."

Proverbs 31:27

As we continue through the chapter, notice that not only should children speak the truth in love, but they should seek ways to be a blessing to their families. Verse twenty-seven says, *"She looketh well to the ways of her household, and eateth not the bread of idleness."* She saw the needs in her home. She explained to her son, "Son, I want you to keep in mind that all of your life you should seek out ways to be a blessing to your family."

It does not matter how old your mother or your father may be or where your sister or brother may be; all throughout life we should seek ways to be a blessing to our families. Be an encouragement to your family.

This mother *"looketh well."* She was always searching out ways to find the needs of her household so that she could be used of God to meet their needs. Let nothing stay between you and another member of your family. Keep the way clear. Keep family ties close.

"Once truth is firmly planted in a child,
it continues steadfastly through any test;
but the planting has to be done early
in the growing season."
–Marcelene Cox

Mother Must Teach Her Children to Succeed at Home

16

"Her children arise up, and call her blessed; her husband also, and he praiseth her."

Proverbs 31:28

Notice an amazing thing. Verse twenty-eight says, *"Her children arise up, and call her blessed; her husband also, and he praiseth her."*

Recently, I was reading the story about a particular lady who was the CEO for Pepsi Cola of America. After much success as a CEO, she walked out of her job and said, "I've had it." She gave up one of the most prestigious jobs any woman has ever had in the history of our nation. She got tired of succeeding everywhere but home.

I pray that ladies who believe they must work will be much more concerned about being a success at home than they are about being a success at work. Determine to succeed at home.

When we read about children doing things they should not do, I hope we do not have this "victim mentality" so deeply ingrained in our thinking that we want to blame someone else. Much blame is wrongly placed on parents. On the other hand, how heartbreaking it is for so many moms and dads to admit that they did not even try to succeed at home.

One of the men who works with me was able to attend a private Christian school as a boy. His mother was willing to clean other people's houses to earn the money necessary to send him to the Christian school. I do not think he resented her for working outside the home in order to provide the proper education for her children.

No doubt the mother in Proverbs chapter thirty-one said to her son, "I would rather a million times over to have my children's love and respect and my husband's love and respect than to have any measure of success outside the home." She taught her son to succeed at home. If in my heart I felt I was failing at home, no measure of worldly success could satisfy my troubled soul.

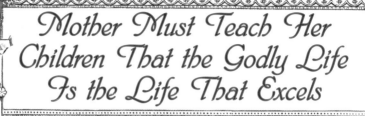

Mother Must Teach Her Children That the Godly Life Is the Life That Excels

17

> *"Many daughters have done virtuously, but thou excellest them all. Favour is deceitful, and beauty is vain: but a woman that feareth the LORD, she shall be praised."*
> Proverbs 31:29-30

he Bible says, *"Many daughters have done virtuously, but thou excellest them all. Favour is deceitful, and beauty is vain: but a woman that feareth the LORD, she shall be praised."* In other words, what are you going to do with your life? She says that a godly life is the life that excels every other life. The one with virtue excels them all.

The question is not "How much do you know?" or "How much have you learned?" or "How much information can you share?" but "Do you have in your heart a desire to live a godly life?" This mother said to her son, "The godly life excels."

My darling mother desired for me to be a pure person. My mother's desire for me to live right and my desire not to disappoint her have gone far in helping me seek to be all I can be for the Lord.

47

"A mother is the only person on earth who can divide her love among ten children and each child still have all her love."

-Unknown

Mother Must Teach Her Children to Keep Their Eyes on the Lord

18

"Favour is deceitful, and beauty is vain: but a woman that feareth the LORD, she shall be praised."

Proverbs 31:30

Keep your eyes on the Lord Jesus Christ. Verse thirty says, *"Favour is deceitful, and beauty is vain: but a woman that feareth the LORD, she shall be praised."* She was talking about a woman, but she was speaking to her son. The best way to go blind in life is to get your eyes on yourself.

What is this generation of young people going to do when they lose the beauty of their youth? What are these young women going to do when they can no longer catch a man with their looks? Shells of human beings are going to be left with immodest dress and faces painted like strange creatures of the night.

It is "sex o'clock" in America and around the world, and many mothers are failing by not telling their daughters what life is really all about. Tell me, what will this generation do when they are cast aside like human wreckage and the beauty of youth has faded like a cut flower? What are they going to do when all they live for is what this world calls beauty and the vanity and deceitfulness of it?

This mother said to her son, "Keep your eyes on the Lord. Fear the Lord." How we need to tell our children to keep their eyes on the Lord Jesus Christ. Fear of the Lord is the beginning of wisdom, and wisdom is what God gives us to make the right decisions in life. Decisions are more important than days. One may live a long life, make wrong decisions, and waste his life, while another may live a short life, make right decisions, and make life a grand success in God's eyes.

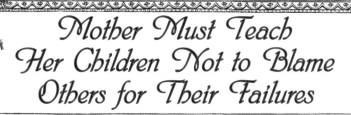

Mother Must Teach Her Children Not to Blame Others for Their Failures

19

"Give her of the fruit of her hands; and let her own works praise her in the gates."

Proverbs 31:31

In verse thirty-one the Bible says, *"Give her of the fruit of her hands; and let her own works praise her in the gates."* She said, "Don't blame other people for your failures."

"Let her own works praise her." If there is one underlying thing that characterizes so many people in our world today, it is that they want to point an accusing finger at others and say, "I didn't have the opportunity. I didn't have the chance. I've been victimized. My dad wasn't what he should have been. My mother wasn't what she should have been."

Do not lean on every excuse in the world for not doing what you should do. What is it God has for you to do? With what are you going to meet Him? You will not be able to blame someone else, though you may try. Why did you not do what you were supposed to do with your life? We all meet God with our own opportunity and ability.

There are certain things that a mother must teach her children. In this chapter, the virtuous woman instructed her son to find a virtuous woman. She knew nothing mattered more than knowing the Lord Jesus Christ as her personal Savior. To know Him we must confess that we are separated from God because of our sin and by faith trust the Lord Jesus who died, was buried, and rose from the dead. If you do not know Him as your personal Savior, trust Him now by asking Him to forgive your sin and inviting Him into your life.

No mother can properly instruct her children without knowing the Lord Jesus Christ as her personal Savior. The indwelling Christ will enable each Christian mother to be the mother He desires for her to be.

Mother Must Teach Her Children How to Know Christ as Savior

20

If our children miss heaven, nothing else they receive in life really matters. There is no age of accountability to God, only a time when a child knows of his lost condition and must trust in Christ and Christ alone for salvation.

Children can and should be saved. The Lord Jesus Christ said in Mark 10:14, *"Suffer the little children to come unto me."* Bring your children to the Lord Jesus Christ. Perhaps the following guideline will help you as you seek to lead your children to Christ.

Realize That God Loves You

God loves you and has a plan for your life.

"For God so loved the world, that he gave his only begotten Son, that whosoever believeth in him should not perish, but have everlasting life."

John 3:16

The Bible Says That All Men Are Sinners

Our sins have separated us from God.

"For all have sinned, and come short of the glory of God."

Romans 3:23

God made man in His own image. He gave man the ability to choose right from wrong. We choose to sin. Our sins keep us from God.

God's Word Also Says That Sin Must Be Paid For

"For the wages of sin is death..."

Romans 6:23

Wages means payment. The payment of our sin is death and hell, separation from God forever. If we continue in our sin, we shall die without Christ and be without God forever.

The Good News Is That Christ Paid for Our Sins

All our sins were laid on Christ on the cross. He paid our sin debt for us. The Lord Jesus Christ died on the cross, and He arose from the dead. He is alive forevermore.

"But God commendeth his love toward us, in that, while we were yet sinners, Christ died for us."

Romans 5:8

We Must Personally Pray and Receive Christ by Faith as Our Savior

"For whosoever shall call upon the name of the Lord shall be saved."

Romans 10:13

Pray and Receive Christ as Your Savior

Lord, I know that I am a sinner. If I died today, I would not go to heaven. Forgive my sin, come into my life and be my Savior. Help me live for You from this day forward. In Jesus' name, Amen

"For whosoever shall call upon the name of the Lord shall be saved."

Romans 10:13

New Life

Everlasting life begins when we receive Christ as our Savior.

A Mother's FAITH

$\mathcal{O}$ne of the most beautiful stories in the Bible illustrating a mother's faith in God is found in Exodus chapter two. Moses stands as a mighty mountain of a man in the Bible; but what we find in the life of Moses, as God raised him up to be the deliverer of Israel, would never have taken place had his mother not had faith in God.

The Bible says in Exodus 2:1-10,

> *And there went a man of the house of Levi, and took to wife a daughter of Levi. And the woman conceived, and bare a son: and when she saw him that he was a goodly child, she hid him three months. And when she could not longer hide him, she took for him an ark of bulrushes, and daubed it with slime and with pitch, and put the child*

55

therein; and she laid it in the flags by the river's brink. And his sister stood afar off, to wit what would be done to him. And the daughter of Pharaoh came down to wash herself at the river; and her maidens walked along by the river's side; and when she saw the ark among the flags, she sent her maid to fetch it. And when she had opened it, she saw the child: and, behold, the babe wept. And she had compassion on him, and said, This is one of the Hebrews' children. Then said his sister to Pharaoh's daughter, Shall I go and call to thee a nurse of the Hebrew women, that she may nurse the child for thee? And Pharaoh's daughter said to her, Go. And the maid went and called the child's mother. And Pharaoh's daughter said unto her, Take this child away, and nurse it for me, and I will give thee thy wages. And the woman took the child, and nursed it. And the child grew, and she brought him unto Pharaoh's daughter, and he became her son. And she called his name Moses: and she said, Because I drew him out of the water.

Make note of one word in this passage. It is a word we all love to speak, one of the most wonderful words in the human languages. It is the closing word found in verse eight. The word is "*mother.*"

Abraham Lincoln said that everything good that happened to him in life came to him because of his darling mother. I thank God for my mother's influence on my life. Mothers need more than one day a year to make special note of their value.

All of us should honor our mothers and fathers. The Bible gives us a commandment with promise, that our days may be long upon the earth as we honor our fathers and mothers. With so many things to look at in this great Bible story, let us consider how the Lord used this mother to accomplish His great purpose in the lives of His people.

Amram took a wife by the name of Jochebed. They were both of the tribe of Levi. Their first child was a daughter, and they named her Miriam. A little later, another child came along. It happened to be a boy. They named him Aaron.

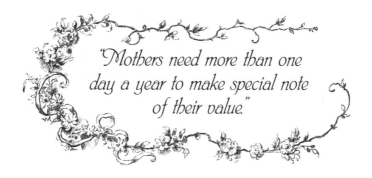

"Mothers need more than one day a year to make special note of their value."

When Aaron was three years old, they had another baby. This little baby caused great joy in their lives, but he also brought tremendous turmoil to their thinking. In between the time of Aaron's birth and this new baby's arrival, a decree was made that all male babies born to the Hebrews must be put to death.

Moses was a special child. As a matter of fact, the Bible tells us he was "exceedingly beautiful." Think about this as we move along in our story. In Acts chapter seven and verse twenty, the Bible says of this man Moses, *"In which time Moses was born, and was exceeding fair, and nourished up in his father's house three months.*" The New Testament records that Moses was "*exceeding fair.*"

We say that all babies are beautiful, and sometimes I think we know we are stretching the truth. It is a wonderful thing that God blesses us with children. But on occasion—I dare not tell you which occasion—it is hard to find any redeeming quality of beauty in the little wrinkled bodies we refer to as babies. We tell every mother with baby in arms, "That is the most beautiful child I've ever seen."

It reminds me of an evangelist friend I have whose mother could not cook well. Everything she tried to cook tasted terrible. He said that on occasion, being an evangelist and going from place to place, he has to eat meals that are not so good. When this happens, he just simply says to the hostess who prepared the meal, "You wouldn't believe this, but your cooking is just like my mother's. It makes me think of her when I eat it."

We figure out some way to get the words out and still rationalize in our minds that we are telling the truth, even if the new baby is not such a beautiful thing to behold.

Moses was a special baby. It is as though God took special pains in making this child beautiful. He knew that when this baby was three months old, special eyes would behold him. Those eyes would have a heart that needed to be strangely moved.

Have you ever seen little girls pick out a doll? We waited twenty-five years to have a girl, and we finally had one—a granddaughter. It is an amazing thing to watch a child pick out a doll and to imagine what they think is most attractive about the little doll.

God made this baby so special that if the daughter of Pharaoh could have picked the little doll she wanted, this would have been the very one. God created this special child and gave Amram and Jochebed this baby boy. God had a mighty work for Moses to do when he grew up. God had a great plan to deliver His people, and this child's life was in every part of it.

THE HATRED OF THE KING

If you could have picked a bad time to have a baby, you could not have picked a worse time than when this baby arrived in Egypt. The decree had been made that any male baby born to the Hebrews had to be thrown into the Nile and killed.

The Word of God tells us by way of review in Exodus 1:1-5,

> *Now these are the names of the children of Israel, which came into Egypt; every man and his household came with Jacob. Reuben, Simeon, Levi, and Judah, Issachar, Zebulun, and Benjamin, Dan, and Naphtali, Gad, and Asher. And all the souls that came out of the loins of Jacob were seventy souls: for Joseph was in Egypt already.*

After the Lord gives a summary, we come to verses six through twelve, and the Bible says,

And Joseph died, and all his brethren, and all that generation. And the children of Israel were fruitful, and increased abundantly, and multiplied, and waxed exceeding mighty; and the land was filled with them. Now there arose up a new king over Egypt, which knew not Joseph. And he said unto his people, Behold, the people of the children of Israel are more and mightier than we: come on, let us deal wisely with them; lest they multiply, and it come to pass, that, when there falleth out any war, they join also unto our enemies, and fight against us, and so get them up out of the land. Therefore they did set over them taskmasters to afflict them with their burdens. And they built for Pharaoh treasure cities, Pithom and Raamses. But the more they afflicted them, the more they multiplied and grew. And they were grieved because of the children of Israel.

The king of Egypt, the Pharaoh, had a plan. Satan had put in his heart a desire to kill the Hebrews. Does it not thrill you to see that the foolishness of God is wiser than men? Does it not thrill you to see that when men think they have some wise plan to work against God, that the God of this universe, our God who lives in our hearts, sits in the heavens and laughs at their wise plans? He knows that it will be brought to foolishness.

The Bible says in verses thirteen through twenty-two,

And the Egyptians made the children of Israel to serve with rigour: and they made their lives bitter

with hard bondage, in mortar, and in brick, and in all manner of service in the field: all their service, wherein they made them serve, was with rigour. And the king of Egypt spake to the Hebrew midwives, of which the name of the one was Shiphrah, and the name of the other Puah: and he said, When ye do the office of a midwife to the Hebrew women, and see them upon the stools; if it be a son, then ye shall kill him: but if it be a daughter, then she shall live. But the midwives feared God, and did not as the king of Egypt commanded them, but saved the men children alive. And the king of Egypt called for the midwives, and said unto them, Why have ye done this thing, and have saved the men children alive? And the midwives said unto Pharaoh, Because the Hebrew women are not as the Egyptian women; for they are lively, and are delivered ere the midwives come in unto them. Therefore God dealt well with the midwives: and the people multiplied, and waxed very mighty. And it came to pass, because the midwives feared God, that he made them houses. And Pharaoh charged all his people, saying, Every son that is born ye shall cast into the river, and every daughter ye shall save alive.

Pharaoh tried to make their work so grievous that it would destroy them. Then he said to the midwives, "When you see a baby boy delivered of a Hebrew woman, kill him immediately." The midwives feared God and would not do it.

Then Pharaoh moved to the next step and said, "If that doesn't work, then I will command that these baby boys be thrown into the river or fed to the beasts. All of them are to be put to death."

No doubt many, perhaps more than we can imagine in number, were taken while mothers pleaded for their little lives. It was a horrible time to rear a child, especially a boy.

Mothers and fathers, be an example to your children in word and deed.

I am reminded of what I hear people saying in this day and hour. "It's a difficult time to rear a baby. It is a difficult time to have a child. Who would want to bring up a baby in a world like the one in which we now live?"

Even Christian people are heard saying, "Well, we're going to get married, but we don't plan to have children because we don't want children to grow up in this kind of world."

Here is a question for you. If God's people do not have children and rear them to fear the Lord and live for God, where are God-fearing people going to come from? May the Lord help us to realize that He has designed the Christian home. He has established the family unit, not simply a "caring unit," as the government has defined the family, but the family unit that God has ordained in Scripture.

The Christian home that God desires us to have becomes a place where we can bring our children to know the Lord, love the Lord, and live for the Lord. It becomes a place to make their lives count for the Lord even though everything in the world seems to be against them.

In Colossians chapter two, the Bible says in verse eight, *"Beware lest any man spoil you through philosophy and vain deceit, after the tradition of men, after the rudiments of the world, and not after Christ."* We need to be aware of these things which are not after Christ.

Mothers and fathers, be an example to your children in word and deed. Has it ever occurred to you that parents are going to reap what they sow in attitude, in word, and in deed? May the

Lord help us to live godly lives before our children. Forsake the things in your home and in your personal life that are not after Christ before they show up in your children. Tell the truth. Speak no guile.

These are difficult—but not impossible—days to rear children to love and serve the Lord. It takes a special concentrated effort on the part of God's people to realize that we live in a world that is at war against God. Beware of the media. Beware of the television. Beware of the children's cartoons. Beware of the little books you buy for your children containing hidden messages of a philosophy that is against God. Beware of the anti-Christ philosophy in secular education.

There is a hatred against Christ. It is not against religion. It is not simply against believing there is a God. The Devil who stirred up the heart of Pharaoh against God's people is the same Devil who stirs up the hearts of people against God's people today.

We cannot conduct business as usual. There must be a concentrated effort on the part of discerning Christian parents to work for Christ with all their hearts in a world that hates our Savior.

THE HEART OF HIS MOTHER

Let us visit the home of this biblical mother and look closely at her heart. Her husband loves her, and she loves him. They have a daughter who is old enough to help them with the little ones.

There is a three-year-old boy running around in the hut in which they dwell. His name is Aaron; someday he will become the high priest. Then there is a little baby, a newborn boy whose life is in grave danger.

One cannot find a more beautiful baby among the Hebrews than the baby born to Amran and Jochebed; but he is a boy, a baby boy sentenced to death by the king.

The parents weep tears of joy, but they also have troubled hearts wondering what to do with their little boy. For three months they have a baby in their home that they are not supposed to have. He cries and wants to be fed, and he gets fussy when he has certain needs. Three months is a long time to hide a baby, especially when baby boys are being searched for by the enemy.

Mother does her best. For three months, she holds onto that child. For three months, she does everything necessary to keep him hidden. For three months, she hovers over him; but then she knows she has to let him go. Her heart is filled with emotion only a mother could understand.

God gives her a plan. She is going to make a little basket for her baby. She is going to make sure that the basket is watertight. It must float. I do not think anyone has ever made a basket with more tender love and care than this mother. No one has ever cared so much about something being watertight as she cared about that little basket being watertight. No mighty ship builder has ever cared more about his ship not sinking than that mother cared about her basket not sinking.

Then one day, she put her beautiful baby boy in the special basket. She and her daughter went out, perhaps to one of the tributaries along the Nile, and placed that basket in the water, waiting on God to do what only He could do.

The moment the current carried him from her hands beyond her reach was the most difficult moment she had ever faced as a mother. It was then all out of her hands. Suddenly, a peace came over her being. This is the way faith works. God gave her peace that He was going to take care of her baby. How? Well, that is God's business. Our business is to trust Him.

If God has not brought you to the place where you had to give your children to Him in the early years of their lives, I guarantee that sometime in their upbringing He will bring you to a point where you know that you cannot do it by yourself. As hard as we try to protect our children, it is impossible to do it alone.

The other day, Andrew, one of my little grandsons, came into my office calling my name. His daddy said, "Papa's not here." I said, "Oh yes, he is." As soon as Andrew heard my voice, he ran around the corner to greet me. I was seated behind my desk. As he ran to me, he ran directly into the corner of the desk and punctured a place in his face right under his eye that immediately began to bleed. It made me sick.

I thought, "I'm going to make this desk padded. I'm going to bring in styrofoam and put it around all the corners." People coming in for an appointment are going to say, "What's all this about?" And I am going to say, "Don't you worry. That padding is necessary if you're going to be a granddaddy."

No amount of work on our part can fully protect our children. God teaches us throughout our lives to give our children to Him. Giving a child to God is desiring for that child what God desires for that child. He knows best, and He does right!

When I was just a little boy, about six or seven years old, my brother, thirteen months younger, had a terrible case of pneumonia. I remember going to the hospital with my parents and visiting him in the pediatric section of the hospital. My dad, who was a rough and tough guy, was standing beside the bed of my brother. My mother was beside him, and I beside my mother. My father started crying. I remember asking my dad, "Why are you crying?" And he said, "Your brother is getting worse, not better."

That moment, my brother was slipping out of their hands, as far as what they could do for him. It was a golden moment for them to hear about God and what God could do. God brings those golden moments to peoples' lives. They look at them first as black, distressful, stormy times. But on the other end, God says, "Oh no, this is a golden moment for Christ to come and help you and for you to realize you need the Lord in rearing your children." Unfortunately, no one got to my parents at that time with the gospel.

When the mother of Moses walked out there and let her baby go, she was entrusting him to God. We see in her as if it were as big as a billboard sign on the side of the road, "I have faith in God to take care of my baby." Oh how we need faith in God! We need faith in God to trust Him with all of our lives. Look long at the heart of this God-fearing mother.

THE HAND OF GOD

Now we see the hand of God clearly. Where was the baby? You say, "He was among the bulrushes or the papyrus plants at the river's brink." No, he was in the hand of God.

Many dear parents bring their children to us to attend Crown College. But do you know where they really must place them? They must place them in God's hands.

While pastoring the Madison Avenue Baptist Church, I was knocking on doors in Paterson, New Jersey, just a few miles from New York City. I encountered a most thrilling thing. I was going down a certain street knocking on doors, giving people gospel literature, witnessing to them about Christ. A young lady about twenty years of age came to the door of a house in a particular type of neighborhood. I saw from her nationality that she did not "belong" in that neighborhood.

I introduced myself and my visitation partner. Reluctantly, she gave me her name. When she gave me her name, God brought something to my mind from years before. I heard a preacher at the Knoxville Baptist Tabernacle when I was very young and just starting out in the ministry. He was a great old saint of God with the same last name as the young lady standing before me at the door. He had long before gone to heaven.

I said to the young lady, "Is there any way you might be related to a man who pastored a great church in Chicago years ago?" Startled, with big tears coming down her cheeks, she said, "I thought I was getting away. I left home. I thought, 'I'm going to New York. Nobody will know me. Nobody will ever find me.'" She said, "I haven't been here but a few days, and God has let me know today by your coming that He knows right where I am." What a wonderful, loving Lord we have.

I would like to have seen Pharaoh's daughter taking her divinely-directed walk that day. You see, He makes the wrath of men to praise Him. The daughter of the man who said, "Kill them all!" came to the very spot of the basket.

She said to one of her maids, "Go get it. What is that?" They fetched the basket; and just as she opened it, she saw the most beautiful child she had ever seen. God tells us in the New Testament that Moses was *"exceeding fair."* She thought, "I have never seen such a beautiful baby." And on top of that, the Lord pinched the baby, and he cried.

As the tears came to his little eyes, her heart melted. In that moment of emotion, here came Miriam running and saying, "There are some Hebrew women who have lost their babies that could nurse a child. Would you like for me to find one of the Hebrew mothers?" Pharaoh's daughter said, "That's a great idea!"

Miriam went back and got the baby's mother and said, "Mother, guess what! God did it! They want you to come and get your own baby boy. Under the safety of the Pharaoh of

Egypt, they are going to deliver the baby into your arms and let you nurse him until he is weaned, maybe until the time he is three years old, then take him back. You will have him long enough to have a bonding as his mother, so he will never forget who you are and who he is."

There is a God in heaven smiling because Pharaoh said, "We're going to wipe out these people. We're going to put an end to these Hebrews. We're going to do away with God's people!" God said, "Oh yes? The truth is, I have taken great pleasure in putting into your palace the very person who is going to grow up and summon the plagues of Egypt upon this land to deliver My people."

If you do not believe that God is at work, then I do not know what is wrong with your heart. This story tells it all. All these things were placed in motion because a mother, by faith, was willing to obey the Lord.

None of us know what God has for our little boys and girls; but I promise you, He has something so special. He desires His special plan for them through your life, Mother, and through your life, Daddy.

We should be on our faces before God saying, "Lord, use me. I am willing to give up anything that hinders and to take hold of anything that blesses the life of the child that You have given me." Let us trust the Lord with our children.

None of us know what God has for our little boys and girls; but I promise you, He has something so special.

The Story of RIZPAH

"And Rizpah the daughter of Aiah took sackcloth, and spread it for her upon the rock, from the beginning of harvest until water dropped upon them out of heaven, and suffered neither the birds of the air to rest on them by day, nor the beasts of the field by night."

II Samuel 21:10

When I think about mothers, of course, I think about my little mother who was only five feet tall and weighed less than a hundred pounds.

After my mother was just a young girl, she had to leave home. When she and my father were married, I was the first-born followed by my brother and two sisters.

Our mother did special things with us when we were young. Often she would roll us around in a little red wagon. I have many precious memories of my mother. I always knew she loved me.

73

Motherhood is ordained of God and designed by the Lord God Himself for a very special purpose.

In Second Samuel chapter twenty-one, we find a precious story of a mother's love. The Bible says in verses one through fourteen,

> *Then there was a famine in the days of David three years, year after year; and David inquired of the LORD. And the LORD answered, It is for Saul, and for his bloody house, because he slew the Gibeonites. And the king called the Gibeonites, and said unto them; (now the Gibeonites were not of the children of Israel, but of the remnant of the Amorites; and the children of Israel had sworn unto them: and Saul sought to slay them in his zeal to the children of Israel and Judah.) Wherefore David said unto the Gibeonites, What shall I do for you? and wherewith shall I make the atonement, that ye may bless the inheritance of the LORD?*

> *And the Gibeonites said unto him, We will have no silver nor gold of Saul, nor of his house; neither for us shalt thou kill any man in Israel. And he said, What ye shall say, that will I do for you. And they answered the king, The man that consumed us, and that devised against us that we should be destroyed from remaining in any of the coasts of Israel, Let seven men of his sons be delivered unto us, and we will hang them up unto the LORD in Gibeah of Saul, whom the LORD did choose. And the king said, I will*

give them. But the king spared Mephibosheth, the son of Jonathan the son of Saul, because of the LORD's oath that was between them, between David and Jonathan the son of Saul. But the king took the two sons of Rizpah the daughter of Aiah, whom she bare unto Saul, Armoni and Mephibosheth; and the five sons of Michal the daughter of Saul, whom she brought up for Adriel the son of Barzillai the Meholathite: and he delivered them into the hands of the Gibeonites, and they hanged them in the hill

> Motherhood is ordained of God and designed by the Lord God Himself for a very special purpose.

before the LORD: and they fell all seven together, and were put to death in the days of harvest, in the first days, in the beginning of barley harvest.

And Rizpah the daughter of Aiah took sackcloth, and spread it for her upon the rock, from the beginning of harvest until water dropped upon them out of heaven, and suffered neither the birds of the air to rest on them by day, nor the beasts of the *field by night. And it was told David what Rizpah the daughter of Aiah, the concubine of Saul, had done. And David went and took the bones of Saul and the bones of Jonathan his son from the men of Jabesh-gilead, which had stolen them from the street of Bethshan, where the Philistines had hanged them, when the Philistines had slain Saul in Gilboa: And he brought up from thence the bones of Saul and the bones of Jonathan his son; and they gathered the bones of them that were hanged. And the bones of Saul and Jonathan his son buried they in the country of Benjamin in Zelah, in the sepulchre of Kish his father: and they performed all that the king commanded. And after that God was entreated for the land.*

This is the story of Rizpah, the story of a lonely hill and a mother's love.

King David was on the throne of Israel, and there was a famine in the land for three years. Of course, David sought the Lord concerning the reason for the famine. God revealed to the king that it was because of the evil treatment that Saul had given to the Gibeonites.

The Gibeonites were people who lived in the land of Canaan when Joshua was leading the children of Israel. The Gibeonites tricked Joshua. They made themselves look as if they had traveled for a long distance, and Joshua made an oath to them that he would not destroy them. After Joshua had sealed that promise in the name of God, he found out that the Gibeonites were a neighboring people and not people from a great distance. But the oath had been made and God's name had sealed it. Joshua's hands were tied. He could not harm the Gibeonites; he had given God's promise on it.

King Saul, in his zeal, decided that he would remove all the Gibeonites from the land of Israel because they were not Jews. He sought to kill them and remove them from the face of the earth. The anger of God was stirred against Israel and against Saul for what he had done. A famine was sent to the land by the hand of God in order to punish the nation for the sin of their king, Saul.

When David realized what it was all about, he asked the Gibeonites to come to him and requested that they tell him what would recompense for the suffering of their people. They came in to see the king, perhaps with smiles on their faces, and David said, "I have found out what the problem is all about. We have betrayed the promise of God against you. We know we have done wrong. What will it take to make it right?" Even though four hundred years had passed since Israel entered Canaan, Saul had disregarded the treaty Joshua had made with the Gibeonites and had gone out of his way to persecute them. The Gibeonites said, "We do not want any gold. We don't want any wealth from Saul, and you will not have to kill anyone in Israel."

David must have thought, "I'm going to get off easily." He made the mistake of saying, "Whatever it is, I promise you I will give it." Suddenly, their smiles were gone and teeth like wolves' teeth appeared on their faces as they said, "Give us seven sons of King Saul, and we will hang them and let their bodies rot where we hang them." David, left with no choice, said, "So be it."

There were two men in this period of time named Mephibosheth. One was a son of Saul and one was a grandson. As you read the Bible, do not be confused because one Mephibosheth was spared by David, yet the other Mephibosheth was given. Five sons from one union and two others, who were the sons of Rizpah, were given to the Gibeonites.

When these seven men were turned over to the Gibeonites, they took them to Gibeah and hanged them. According to law, they had to hang there without anyone removing their bodies until their bodies had rotted and decayed and the wild beasts of the land had torn the flesh from their bones and the vultures had plucked out their eyes. The mother of two of these boys decided that she was not going to allow that to happen. Her name was Rizpah.

What happened on the hill where their bodies were left to rot forms one of the most moving episodes in the Bible. It also reveals the wild, warlike world that framed the background for so much of the Old Testament.

The Word of God tells us that this woman went to the place where her sons were hanged. She spread a cloth upon the rocks. The Bible also marks the time that these boys were put to death and marks the time that she was allowed to leave when these sons received proper burial.

She was there for at least four months, day and night. In the heat of the day, she would take rags and cloths and run the birds off to keep them from the bodies of her sons. At night, as wolves and wild beasts would come and smell the decaying flesh, wanting to rip the flesh from the bones of her boys, that little woman fought off the animals and would not allow them to touch the bodies of her sons.

For four months, at least, she was there until word of this finally reached King David. When David heard the story of Rizpah and her love for her boys, the king said, "Forget the law. Remove their bodies and go down to the men of Jabesh-gilead and get the bones of King Saul and his son Jonathan. We are going to bury those sons of Rizpah like royalty." David took their bones, along with the bones of Saul and Jonathan, to the land of Benjamin to the sepulcher of Kish, Saul's father, and buried them like royalty.

Why would God include such a story in His Word? He intends for us to have our hearts stirred about the devotion of motherhood. He wants us to see something of the passion of this woman's heart for her children. When we think about her love, we are caused to think about a greater love than hers, the love of our precious Savior who died on Calvary. Look closely at the lonely hill on which the bodies of Saul's sons were left to rot. Why were they there?

THE SINS OF THEIR FATHER

Did they sin? The truth of the matter is, those boys were not there for their sin; they were suffering and dying for the sins of their father.

I know we live in an age where it is fashionable for children to blame all their problems on Mom and Dad. All problems should not be blamed on Mom and Dad, but there are many children who suffer greatly through life because of the sins of their selfish mother and father.

Recently, I read a survey on alcoholism. The article showed descriptive pictures of children whose faces were disfigured, whose lives were wrecked because of the alcoholism of their parents.

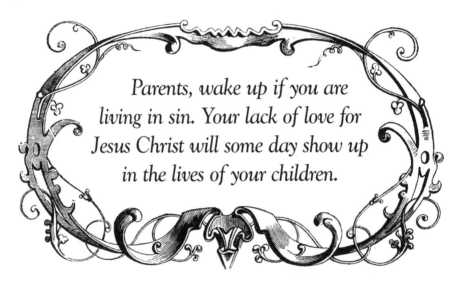

Parents, wake up if you are living in sin. Your lack of love for Jesus Christ will some day show up in the lives of your children.

The entire article was on the destruction caused by alcohol and the horrible consequences world-wide from the use of it. I thought how awful it was that those children had to suffer, and I also thought how cowardly many preachers are today in pulpits across America who do not have the courage to speak out against alcohol. An international magazine will speak out against it, and preachers will not even raise their voices against it. May God help us to have boldness to call sin by name and be unashamed and unafraid to preach the whole counsel of God.

Parents, wake up if you are living in sin. Your lack of love for Jesus Christ will some day show up in the lives of your children. Your lack of devotion to the work of God and the church of the living God will some day wake you up as you see the foul fruit of it in the lives of your own children. May God help us to see our parental responsibility as we look at those sons who were suffering, who were hanged because of the sin of their father.

A Desire for Revenge

Remember, David sent for the elders of the Gibeonites and requested that they tell him what would recompense for the suffering of their people. Nothing would satisfy them but the blood of the surviving sons of King Saul.

David, no doubt horrified, knew that it was useless to argue and said, "I will give them."

The seven remaining sons of Saul were taken and hanged on a hilltop where all the world could see. Seven innocent men were slaughtered because of a desire for revenge.

The Gibeonites were there because they wanted to get even. That is all that mattered to them. They wanted revenge. They did not care who they hurt. They did not care about Rizpah. They did not care about who they affected.

Have you ever thought about how much suffering there is in the world because of people who want to get back at someone? Have you ever thought about how many times a heart is broken because someone would not be quiet when he could have been quiet?

There is no place in the Christian's life for a get-even, get-back spirit. Being willing to forgive someone is giving up our right to get even or get back. If we have any spirit in us that wants to hurt someone or wants to get back at someone because we think he has mistreated us, it is obvious that this is not the spirit of Jesus Christ.

The desire of the Gibeonites was to kill the sons of Saul. They had an evil spirit. May God help us to come to the Savior and say, "Lord, forgive me, cleanse me. Help me to leave those things in Your hands, not to go through life as if it were my responsibility to seek revenge on everyone I think has wronged me or wronged someone I love." May God give us the faith and the grace to leave these things in the hands of the Lord.

The old adage is true that the vessel that contains poison is also affected by the poison. If we have bitterness or unforgiveness in our hearts, it may be vented toward someone else, but you and I both know it is going to have a terribly destructive effect on us.

THE LOVE OF THEIR MOTHER

The Gibeonites wanted revenge. But what about Rizpah? What about this beautiful picture of motherhood? Why was she there? She was there because she loved her sons.

There is a greater love than Mother's love, but there has been many a boy changed because of Mother's love. There is a greater love than Father's love, but there has been many a boy and many a girl reached through Mama and Daddy loving them.

C. T. Studd, the great missionary, said when he left in a rage one day, never to serve God, never to honor God, that his father tried to reason with him. He did everything he could to reason with him, to use logic on him. C. T. Studd said, "It was easy for me to escape my father's logic." But he said, "All my mother did was stand there and weep." He said, "So help me God, I could never escape my mother's tears. They brought me to the Lord."

I remember my little mother sitting with me on the side of the bed and saying, "I'm raising you without a father. I've put a lot of responsibility on you." She said, "We are not getting along. You

> *"I could never escape my mother's tears. They brought me to the Lord."*
> – C.T. Studd

know it, son. I need you. Our home needs you. I believe God is going to deal with you if you don't do what you are supposed to do."

She said this with a broken heart. I want you to know that I could not get away from her tears. Before I could ever serve the Lord, I sat down as an eighteen-year-old boy and wrote my mother a letter saying, "Mother, I know I have broken your heart, but I have made things right with God and have asked God to forgive me and to help me. I promise you, and I promise God from this day forward, as long as God allows me to live, I'll make you happy to say that I am your son." I meant what I said that day, and I mean it now.

The Mercy of Our Savior

When we think about Rizpah and we think about how much she loved those boys to stay out there month after month, day after day, fighting off animals, beating back birds, I want you to know there is a greater love that is wooing you today. It is the love of Jesus Christ.

Rizpah's vigil for her son, who were slain for the sins of another, reminds us of Mary's vigil at the foot of the cross where the Lord Jesus Christ suffered, bled, and died for the sins of the world, your sins and mine.

Jesus Christ came from heaven's glory, paid our sin debt on the cross, bore the awful weight of our sin, suffered, bled and died for us. The billows of God's wrath rolled on Him. He paid the debt for us on that cross so that the holiness of God could be satisfied and we could come to the Lord and ask for mercy and forgiveness. The way has been made plain. We can come to the Lord Jesus and say, "God help me, forgive me, and cleanse me. Help me to be all I should be, all You want me to be."

Through this story of a mother's love, I pray today that you will respond to the love of the Lord Jesus Christ.

THE GOOD-NIGHT KISS

Always send your little child to bed happy. Whatever cares may trouble your mind, give the dear child a warm good-night kiss as he goes to his pillow. The memory of this, in the stormy years which may be in store for the little one, will be like Bethlehem's star to the bewildered shepherds; and welling up in the heart will rise the thought: "My father and my mother loved me!" Lips parched with fever will become dewy again at this thrill of useful memories. Kiss your little child before he goes to sleep.

– Anonymous

For this child I prayed;
and the LORD hath
given me my petition
which I asked of him:
Therefore also I have
lent him to the LORD;
as long as he liveth
he shall be lent to
the LORD.

———

I SAMUEL 1:27-28

Mother's Day

Mother's Day, as we know it, originated with Anna M. Jarvis. She was never blessed with children of her own but missed her own dear mother so much that she caused the establishment of a national holiday. Miss Jarvis' mother, also named Anna, had once promoted the idea of "Mother's Friendship Days" as a way to unite the country. In memory of her mother, Anna M. Jarvis persuaded the Andrews Methodist Church of Grafton, West Virginia, to hold a Sunday service on the anniversary of her passing-May 10, 1908. The governor of West Virginia proclaimed Mother's Day as a state holiday in 1910, and in 1914, Congress and President Woodrow Wilson each issued nationwide proclamations designating the second Sunday in May as an official national holiday.

THE SEXTONS
1950'S FAMILY PHOTOGRAPH

Preston and Ruby Sexton, and family (clockwise from left), Tommy, Sheila, Clarence, and Katherine. This photograph was taken in 1955 at the East Lake Courts Housing Project in Chattanooga, Tennessee. At this time, the children rode the Sunday School bus to Highland Park Baptist Church where Dr. Lee Roberson was the pastor.

A Mother's Love

By D. L. Moody

The closest tie on earth is a mother's love for her child. There are a good many things that will separate a man from his wife; but there isn't a thing in the wide, wide world that will separate a true mother from her own child. I will admit that there are unnatural mothers, that there are mothers who are so steeped in sin and iniquity that they will turn against their own children. I have talked with mothers when my blood boiled with indignation against the sons for their treatment of their mothers, and I have said, "Why don't you cast him off?"

They have said, "Why, Mr. Moody, I love him still. He is my son."

I was once preaching for Dr. G. in St. Louis, and when I got through, he said that he wanted to tell me a story. There was a boy who was very bad. He had a very bad father who seemed to take delight in teaching his son everything that was bad. The father died, and the boy went on from bad to worse until he was arrested for murder.

When he was on trial, it came out that he had murdered five other people, and from one end of the city to the other there was a universal cry going up against him. During his trial they had to guard the courthouse, the indignation was so intense.

The white-haired mother got just as near her son as she could, and every witness that went into the court and said anything against him seemed to hurt her more than her son. When the jury brought in a verdict of guilty, a great shout went up; but the old mother nearly fainted away; and when the judge pronounced the sentence of death, they thought she would faint away.

After it was over, she threw her arms around him and kissed him, and there in the court they had to tear him from her embrace. She then went the length and breadth of the city trying to get men to sign a petition for his pardon. And when he was hanged, she begged the governor to let her have the body of her son, that she might bury it. They say that death has torn down everything in this world, everything but a mother's love. That is stronger than death itself. The governor refused to let her have the body, but she cherished the memory of that boy as long as she lived.

A few months later, she followed her boy in death, and when she was dying, she sent word to the governor and begged that her body might be laid close to her son. That is a mother's love! She wasn't ashamed to have her grave pointed out for all time as the grave of the mother of the most noted criminal the State of Vermont ever had.

The prophet takes hold of that very idea. He says, *"Can a mother forget her child?"* But a mother's love is not to be compared to the love of God.

ABOUT THE AUTHOR

Clarence Sexton's ministry began in east Tennessee where he served as a pastor for seven years. He then joined Dr. Lee Roberson at Highland Park Baptist Church in Chattanooga and served there for five years as an assistant pastor. During the following eight years, Dr. Sexton pastored Madison Avenue Baptist Church located 11 miles west of New York City. Clarence Sexton became the pastor of the Temple Baptist Church of Powell, Tennessee, in August of 1988.

The ministries of Temple Baptist Church have grown steadily under the direction of Dr. Sexton. For many years, Pastor Sexton had a burden to begin a college that would train Christian men and women as they prepared to serve the Lord with their lives. This burden became a reality when The Crown College opened in August of 1991. At present, more than 900 students come from every state and several foreign countries to attend the college. In addition to the work of The Crown College, Pastor Sexton serves as the publisher of *The Baptist Vision* and the FAITH *for the* FAMILY Journal.

Clarence Sexton has been in the ministry of the Lord Jesus Christ since 1967. He has written more than thirty-five books and booklets. He speaks in conferences throughout the United States and has conducted training sessions for pastors and Christian workers in several countries around the world. He and his wife Evelyn have been married for forty years. They have two grown sons and six grandchildren. For more information, visit us at www.FAITH*forthe*FAMILY.com.

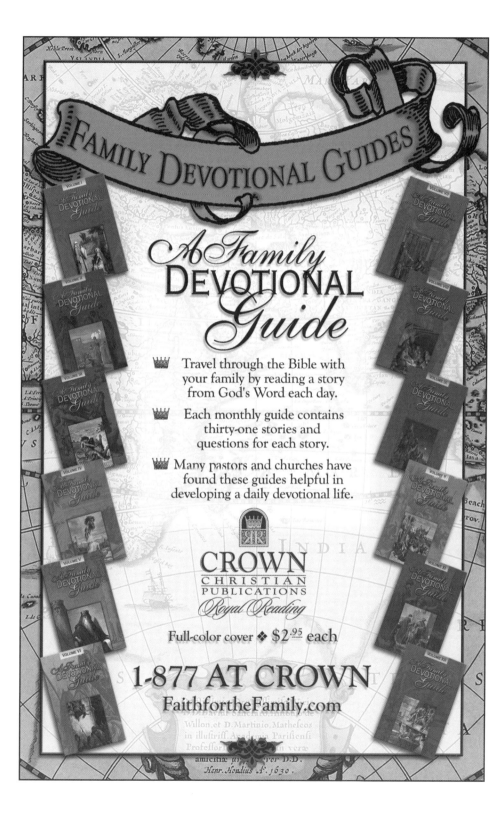